HAVELOK THE WARRIOR

The King of England had a daughter whose name was Goldborough, and she was the fairest and loveliest creature in the land. When she was twenty-years-old she fell victim to the evil schemes of Godric, Earl of England, who had taken her father's place. She was cast into the dungeons of Dover Castle and there left while Godric plotted to steal her throne.

But Havelok the Dane was in the land, and fate was to take a hand in uniting Havelok and Goldborough against the cruel men who had stolen their kingdoms . . .

3bcd

Ian Serraillier

Havelok the Warrior

Illustrated by Gareth Floyd

CAROUSEL EDITOR: ANNE WOOD

TRANSWORLD PUBLISHERS LTD
A NATIONAL GENERAL COMPANY

HAVELOK THE WARRIOR

A CAROUSEL BOOK 0 552 52007 1

Originally published in Great Britain
by Hamish Hamilton Ltd.

PRINTING HISTORY

Hamish Hamilton edition published 1968
Carousel edition published 1971

Carousel Books are published by Transworld Publishers Ltd.,
Cavendish House, 57–59 Uxbridge Road, Ealing, London W.5

Made and printed in Great Britain by
Richard Clay (The Chaucer Press), Ltd., Bungay, Suffolk.

To Philip

AUTHOR'S NOTE

The Lay of Havelok the Dane was one of the metrical romances that were popular in England between 1200 and 1500. These were stories of adventure and strange and marvellous deeds, in which kings and queens and knights and ladies played heroic parts. *The Lay of Havelok* was written in rhyming couplets in the Lincolnshire dialect about 1300, and the only known manuscript is housed in the Bodleian Library, Oxford. The poem was probably composed by one of the many minstrels who wandered up and down the country to sing in castle and market place. The simple style, the homely imagery, and the poet's obvious sympathy with humble folk suggest that it was written for them and not for the upper classes, who in those days spoke mainly French. This version follows the story fairly closely, but it is not a word-by-word translation.

How much of the story is true? Most of it is clearly legend and folktale, but Havelok himself may be based on a real person. A thirteenth-century chronicler claimed that he was the son of the Danish invader Guthrum, who was defeated in battle by Alfred the Great in 878. Modern scholars have tried to connect him with famous Vikings like Olaf Sictrison or King Sweyn of Denmark, who seized the English crown after subduing the country in 1013. The two places most closely connected with Havelok —Lincoln and Grimsby—were obviously familiar to the unknown poet. The ancient Town Seal of Grimsby is engraved with the armed figure of Grim the fisherman, as well as with Havelok and Goldborough, both of whom are shown wearing crowns. Legends about them lingered on in the district for several centuries. But nobody can be at all certain about their historical basis, and it is mainly for the quality of the storytelling that the poem is still remembered.

ONE

They wrung their hands, wept bitter tears—
In vain he tried to calm their fears.

Once there was a King of England named Athelwold, a God-fearing man who made good laws and saw that they were kept. During his reign England was so safe that a man could travel the length of the land with fifty pounds of gold on his back and no risk of being robbed. If a beggar knocked at his door, he gave him the finest roast meat and the choicest dishes from his table. Anyone caught harming an orphan or a widow he bound in chains and threw into prison. Outlaws and thieves he hanged on the gallows, and neither silver nor gold could save them. In battle against his enemies he was like the spark of fire that leaps from the living coal. They threw up their hands and howled for mercy, or crept into corners to hide. No wonder he was loved by good men everywhere.

Suddenly he was taken gravely ill. He could neither eat nor sleep. As he lay on his sick-bed at Winchester, in great pain and near to death, he

cried out, 'What will happen to my only child, my daughter Goldborough? She is motherless and I am afraid for her. If only she were old enough to be Queen or to ride on horseback with a thousand men at her side, I could die happy. But she is still too young to walk or speak. Oh, what am I to do?'

He decided to consult his nobles. So he summoned to his bedside every earl and baron between Roxburgh and Dover.

At last they arrived. As they crowded sadly around his bed, he welcomed them and tried to comfort them.

'Your tears cannot help me, for I am dying,' he

said. 'Pray for my daughter, who will be your lady when I am no longer here. She is still too young to be Queen. Who is to look after her and rule England until she comes of age?'

'Earl Godric of Cornwall is your man,' they answered. 'He is wise and highly respected. You can trust him.'

Earl Godric stepped forward and knelt by the bed.

'Earl Godric,' said the King, 'you must swear on the holy books to watch over my child with loving care. As soon as she is old enough to think of marriage, you must find the tallest, the best, the strongest, and most handsome man alive. Then marry her to him and have her crowned Queen of England.'

When Earl Godric had taken the oath, Goldborough was carried in by her nurse. Her locks were as pale as primroses, her fists as small as fern-leaves before they uncurl.

'I give her into your keeping, together with all my lands,' said the King. 'She is my only child. Treat her kindly.'

The Earl lifted her up and held her fondly in his arms.

Then the King made his will. He gave away all his money and possessions. Not a penny was left, not even enough to pay for his winding-sheet. Priests gave him the last sacrament and heard his confession. As the colour faded from his cheeks, he cried, 'Into Thy hands, O Lord!'

And his tongue was silent forever.

Sadly the church bells tolled as his body was laid to rest in the earth. And all England—lords and ladies in their castles, peasants in the fields, rich and poor alike—mourned him.

TWO

I clothed and fed her. Why should she
Be Queen and lady over me?

Earl Godric at once took control of the country. Everyone, friend and foe alike, swore allegiance to him. He appointed new judges, handed over the castles to knights he could trust, and instructed sheriffs and officers to keep the woods free from bandits. But so harsh was his justice and so cruel was he to his prisoners that soon all England feared him, as a dog fears the whip.

Meanwhile Goldborough grew up happily. She was gracious, well-mannered, and sensible. By the time she was twenty years old, there was no lovelier lady in the land. But because she was heir to the kingdom, Earl Godric was jealous of her.

'I have brought her up too softly,' he muttered. 'I have fed and clothed her too well, and she has grown too proud. Why should she be Queen over me? Why should she have all England—me and mine as well—in her hand? I

have a son of my own, a gallant boy. I'd give my life to see him made King and master.'

This traitor no longer cared a straw for his promises. He seized Goldborough and dragged her off to Dover, where a grim castle stands on the

cliff and guards the sea. Dressing her in rags like a beggar, he threw her into the dungeon. He refused to let any of her friends go near her.

And there, as she lies weeping on the cold flagstones, we must leave her for a while.

THREE

Is there no corn to make us bread,
No water to drink? We are nearly dead.

In those days the mighty Birkabeyn was King of Denmark. Rich and handsome, he was the bravest general that rode a horse or hurled a spear. He had three fine children, a son and two daughters, whom he loved dearly. But while still in the prime of life he was, like Athelwold, taken mortally ill.

Priests at his bedside gave him the last sacrament. He made his will and gave away all his possessions. Then, turning to the lords and barons gathered around his bed, he cried out, 'I am deeply anxious for my children. Which of you will look after them until they are old enough to go riding with knights at their side?'

'Earl Godard is your man,' they answered. 'There is no braver knight, no truer friend under the moon.'

Godard stepped forward and knelt down. In simple trust the King laid his hand on the Earl's head.

'I give my three children into your keeping,' he said. 'Swear by the sacred altar that you will bring them up with selfless care. When my son is of age, old enough to march with spear and helmet at the head of his army, swear that you will crown him King. Denmark and all that goes with it—the towns and castles, the woods and rolling fields—are now his.'

Godard took the oath, and soon afterward King Birkabeyn died.

The boy was the eldest of the three children, and his name was Havelok. His sisters, bright-eyed Swanborow and Helfled of the golden hair, were little more than babies, not yet three winters old. No sooner was their father buried than Godard threw them into prison. He gave them rags to wear and rags to sleep on. He did not care a nut for his promises—he was a man with ice in his heart.

One evening he climbed the stairway to the turret where they were imprisoned. He slid the bolts and opened the door.

Havelok knelt and greeted him.

'Why do you keep weeping and howling?' Godard snarled.

'We are starving,' said Havelok. 'No knight or page comes near this dismal place. Is there no corn to make bread, no water?'

Godard listened but he answered not a word. He looked at the little girls—their cheeks were green with hunger. He picked them up gently,

as if to fondle them. Then he killed them.

Havelok shut his eyes in terror. When he opened them, he saw Godard's knife pointed at his heart.

'Be merciful, my lord!' he sobbed. 'I'll give you all Denmark, if you will let me live. I'll never lift sword or spear against you. I'll leave Denmark forever. Oh, my lord, be merciful!'

For a brief moment a spark of pity flashed in Godard's heart. He could not kill Havelok with his own hands. But as he stared at the boy, his mind was angrily scheming: 'If I let him go, I shall never be safe. He's sure to seek me out and kill me. But once he is dead my children can be lords of Denmark after me. . . . I will get someone else to do the deed.'

FOUR

She brought him bread and cheese and meat—
Heartily he began to eat.

Godard did not waste a moment. He sent at once for a fisherman he knew and had him brought to the prison. The man's name was Grim, and he had a hill of dark hair and brows like bushes.

'Grim, you know you are my slave,' said Godard. 'Would you like me to set you free? Would you like to be rich? Then listen and do as I tell you. You see this boy—he is a traitor's son. Take him back with you now. Tie an anchor around his neck, and when the moon rises throw him into the sea and drown him.'

Grim tied up the boy with the toughest rope that he could find. He gagged him with a filthy rag, so tightly that he could hardly breathe. He picked up an old sack from the floor and bundled Havelok inside. Then, heaving the sack over his shoulder, he carried it home to his cottage by the sea.

He handed the sack to his wife, Dame Leve.

'Guard this boy like gold,' he told her. 'If you let him escape, Lord Godard will kill you.'

'What are you going to do with him?'

'Drown him,' said Grim. 'In return Lord Godard has promised to set us free, and we shall be rich for the rest of our lives.'

Dame Leve was trembling so much that she dropped the sack, uncovering Havelok's head, which struck the stone floor.

'Oh, I wish I had never been born a King's son,' thought the boy. 'Treacherous Godard! Why has no wolf from the wild lands made off with him? Why has no eagle swept down from the sky and torn him with his talons?'

While Havelok lay on the cold floor, Grim and his wife retired to bed. Their five young children—three sons and two daughters—had not woken and were sleeping peacefully. But Dame Leve was so troubled that she could not rest. She pleaded with her husband not to drown the boy.

'I made a promise to Lord Godard,' he said. 'Does my word of honour mean nothing to you? Look, the moon is rising from the sea. Get up, and blow the fire and light a candle.'

Dame Leve picked up her husband's clothes and laid them for him on the bed. Then she bent down to blow the fire.

Suddenly she looked around. The boy had slipped out of the sack and was lying in a pool of light, a shaft of brightness streaming from his

mouth. It seemed as if the room were lit by a hundred glittering candles.

Grim sprang out of bed, and they both ran to the boy. They ungagged him, cut the rope, and rolled back his shirt. On his right shoulder they found a shining mark. It was the birthmark of a King, proof that he must be Birkabeyn's son and heir to Denmark. They knew that their allegiance was to Havelok now, and not to Godard.

Grim fell on his knees at Havelok's feet and buried his head in his hands. 'Lord Havelok, have mercy on us,' he begged. 'We are your slaves, and only you can set us free. We shall look after you and feed you till you are old enough to ride a horse and wear armour. All Denmark shall be yours, and Godard shall be hanged.'

Though the rope had bitten deep into Havelok's flesh and the gag had nearly choked him, he managed to smile. He sat up and asked for something to eat. Dame Leve ran and fetched him bread and cheese, butter and milk, meat pies and cheese flans.

'Thank God you can still swallow,' she said, as she watched him eating heartily. He ate a whole loaf, for he had had nothing for three days.

Then Grim made up a bed for him, undressed him, and tucked him in.

'Sleep soundly, my son,' he said. 'You have nothing to be afraid of now.'

FIVE

Make me rich, my lord, and free,
As yesterday you promised me.

Next day at dawn Grim went straight to Godard.

'Have you obeyed my orders?' said Godard.

'My lord, I tied an anchor to the boy's neck and drowned him. I have come for my reward.'

'So you think that crime should be rewarded?' sneered Godard. 'You think a murderer should be made an earl?'

'My lord, you promised me riches and freedom. That is all I ask for.'

'You have always been a slave,' said Godard, 'and you shall remain one until your dying day. That is your reward! Get out of my sight before I have you hanged!'

Grim ran home as fast as his legs would carry him. He realized that if Godard found out that Havelok was still alive, he and his wife would be hanged. Their only hope was to leave Denmark. So he sold all the possessions that his success as a fisherman had brought him—his

corn, his sheep and goats, his horses and cattle, his pigs and geese and hens. Whatever he could turn into money he parted with. He overhauled his boat, tarring the seams with pitch so that she would not leak. He fitted a new mast, new sail, oars, and cables. As soon as everything was ready, he went on board with Havelok and his wife and children and steered for the open sea.

They were a mile from the coast when a north wind sprang up and followed them to England. Little did Havelok know what dangers lay before him there, or what suffering and sorrow he was to endure.

SIX

God grant that I may soon repay
The hands that fed me till today.

Grim landed on the east coast of England, near the mouth of the Humber. His ship ran aground on the sand, and he hauled it ashore. While he was building a house of earth, he used the sail to make a temporary shelter. The place where they settled he called Grimsby, and it has kept the name to this day.

At once he set about earning his living as a fisherman. He found there were great shoals of herring swimming around the coast, and they were not difficult to catch. He also caught cod and porpoise, mackerel, flat-fish, plaice and skate, sturgeon, turbot, salmon, and even seal and whale. He put wicker traps in the river to catch eels. All the fish he caught were salted and packed, ready to be sold. Then he and his three sons filled their baskets, strapped them to their backs, and disappeared into the towns and villages to sell their wares. In Lincoln they would walk all over the town to get the best prices. With-

the takings they bought bread made from the finest flour and three-cornered simnel cakes, which Grim stuffed into his shirt and cloak to carry home. Then they filled their baskets with beans and corn, beef, mutton and pork, and sometimes with rope for making fishing nets as well. They never returned home empty-handed.

For twelve winters Grim and his household prospered.

Meanwhile Havelok had grown into a strong and lusty youth. He could eat more than Grim and his five children together, so Grim was hard put to it to earn enough to keep them all. But because Havelok was a King's son, Grim did not expect him to help.

Havelok did not agree. He thought the time had come for him to do his share. 'I am not a child now, and there is nothing to be ashamed of in hard work,' he said. 'A man who wants to eat and drink well has no business to be lazing about at home. My back can carry a basket of fish as well as anyone else's. If it's as heavy as a tree trunk, it won't hurt me. I shall start work tomorrow.'

Next morning he got up at sunrise, filled his basket with enough fish for four ordinary loads, then strapped it to his back and marched off to Lincoln alone. He sold the lot, and every silver piece he earned he brought home. He did not keep a penny for himself. In a week or two he knew the trade as well as Grim or his sons.

Yet, in spite of his help, the family's good fortune did not last. The thirteenth winter brought famine to the land. There was a great shortage of corn and bread, and even the sea seemed empty of fish. As Havelok had so huge an appetite, Grim could not help being anxious about him. Besides, he loved him with all his heart.

'Havelok, my dear son,' he said, 'there's not a crumb of bread in the house. Go to Lincoln and find work before it is too late.'

'How can I go, Father? My clothes are in rags.'

'I will make you a cloak from the sail,' said Grim.

He took down his shears from a hook and cut out a cloak for Havelok. There was nothing left to make an undershirt or hose, or to wrap around his feet for shoes. But at least the cloak would keep him from freezing to death.

'God bless you, my son,' said Grim. There were tears in his eyes as he stood at the door and said good-bye.

'God bless you, too,' said Havelok.

He set off barefoot along the icy rutted tracks to Lincoln.

SEVEN

All people loved him, young and old,
Knights and children, shy and bold.

When he arrived in Lincoln, Havelok felt as lost and bewildered as a ploughboy in a palace. There was no work to be had, and for two days he had nothing to eat. On the third day he was standing in a crowd of workless labourers as poor as himself, when he heard a man on the steps of the market cross shouting, 'Porters! Porters!' It was Bertram, the Earl of Cornwall's cook.

Nine or ten men sprang forward, but Havelok was so eager to get work that he knocked them flying and left them sprawling in the mud. Impressed by his strength, Bertram told him to go with him to the bridge.

On the bridge stood a chapel, a house or two, and some shops, where Bertram stopped to buy food for the Earl's larder. He crammed it all into Havelok's basket and told him to carry it up the steep hill to the castle. At the gate Bertram dismissed him, tossing him a half-penny loaf for his wages.

Next morning Havelok hung about the market place, hoping that the cook would return. When he failed to appear, Havelok did not lose hope. He went straight to the bridge, and there he found Bertram standing by a pile of fish he had just bought. He was shouting for porters.

Havelok sprang forward—and anyone who stood in his way got a fist in his face. He laid out more than sixteen lads, then ran up to the cook and began to fill his basket with fish from the heap. Salmon, plaice, cuttlefish, eels, huge lampreys—there were enough to fill a cart, but he picked up the lot and marched cheerfully up the hill to the castle. In the kitchen the servants helped him down with the load.

'Would you like to stay and work for me?' said Bertram, with a grin of admiration.

'Gladly,' said Havelok.

'I can give you your keep.'

'That's all the payment I ask,' said Havelok. 'In return I'll fetch in fuel and water, chop the wood, kindle the fire and make it roar in the chimney place. I can skin eels and wash the dishes too. I'll do anything you want.'

'Good,' said Bertram. 'Now sit on the bench there and let me see you eat.'

There was a huge pot of broth on the fire, and on the table a loaf as long as Havelok's arm. By the time Havelok had finished there was nothing left—not a crumb of bread, not a spoonful of broth.

'I have never seen such an appetite,' said Bertram.

'But I have strength to match it,' said Havelok. 'I mean to earn my keep, I promise you.'

He went out into the yard. Beside the well there was a tub large enough for a giant's bath. Havelok filled it with water, heaved it on to his back, and carried it into the kitchen. Everyone was amazed.

So Havelok became a kitchen boy. Whatever he did, whether it was fetching food from the bridge or carrying in fuel and water, he never needed any help from anyone. He was as strong and tireless as an ox.

Yet for all his gifts he was the humblest of men. Always cheerful and merry, he never worried other people with his troubles. Children loved him, for he was full of fun and would play with them for hours on end. In fact there was no one, young or old, high or low, who did not love him. Everywhere people were remarking how big and strong he was, how gentle—and how handsome, except for his clothes. The cloak that Grim had made for him was now in shreds and filthy. When Bertram, out of kindness of his heart, bought him new clothes and shoes, in all England there was not a man as brave and handsome as Havelok. He looked every inch a King.

EIGHT

Marry this man, or understand
That I shall sweep you from the land.

In those days parliament used to meet in different cities in turn. Soon it was the turn of Lincoln. Earl Godric, the ruler of England, summoned his earls and barons to assemble there. As it was usual for games to be held there at the same time, many champions came too, as well as crowds of spectators from all over the country—servants, grooms, ploughboys, priests, and parsons, as well as the Earl's men.

One of the games was putting the stone—a stone as heavy as an ox. Only the toughest could lift it to his knees. Nobody could lift it to his chest, and anyone who could hurl it a few feet was hailed as a champion.

Havelok was watching with the crowd. Although he stood head and shoulders above the rest, it did not occur to him to take part, as he knew nothing whatever about the sport. When Bertram told him to have a go, after much hesitation he agreed.

To everyone's amazement, at the very first throw he hurled the stone twelve feet farther than anybody else.

'It's time we were going,' said the champions, nudging each other and laughing. They knew it was no good trying to improve on Havelok's throw.

The news of this extraordinary feat spread quickly to every hall and castle in the land. Godric, who was already in Lincoln, was one of the first to hear it. At once he began scheming.

'Did I not promise Athelwold that his daughter should marry the tallest, the strongest, and the most handsome man alive? This scullion, this kitchen boy shall be her husband,' he

sneered. 'If I searched as far as India, I could find no one to suit my purpose better. England would never accept a kitchen boy as King. I shall be able to keep the throne for myself, and for my son after me, and bring disgrace on Goldborough. Not an inch of English ground shall be hers.'

Such was his treacherous plan, although by rights the whole land belonged to Goldborough.

He had her brought at once to Lincoln. All the church bells were ringing as she rode through the streets.

'Goldborough, I have a husband for you,' he told her when she arrived at the castle. 'He is the most handsome man in the world.'

'What do I care how handsome he is?' she cried. 'Unless he is a King or a King's son, I shall refuse to marry him.'

Godric sprang to his feet, trembling with anger. 'Do you think you can give orders to *me*?' he shouted. 'I tell you, *I* am master here. You shall marry the man I have chosen.'

'Sir, you have not told me his rank. Is he a King's son?'

'He is a kitchen boy, and you shall marry him tomorrow.'

Ashamed and horrified, Goldborough burst into tears.

Next morning at sunrise, while the priests were ringing the bells for matins, Godric sent for Havelok and asked him bluntly if he wanted a wife.

'A wife, sir? What in heaven's name should I do with a wife? I have no money to feed and clothe her. And where would she live? I have no home. I have no possessions of my own—not a twig, a stick, or a breadcrumb, and no garment except a ragged old cloak too dirty to wear. Even the clothes I am wearing are not my own. They belong to my master, the cook.'

Godric took a horsewhip and began to beat him. 'I have chosen a wife for you,' he shouted. 'And if you don't accept her, I'll put out your eye! I'll hang you on the nearest tree!'

A ring on his finger or a noose around his neck—which was it to be? Reeling from the blows, Havelok cried out that he would do as Godric wished.

Then Godric sent for Goldborough.

'Here is your kitchen boy,' he sneered. 'If you refuse to marry him, I shall sweep you from the land.'

Lying bruised and battered on the ground, Havelok looked up at Goldborough. She was as pale as a flower that has grown in darkness and never seen the sun. Dizzy with pain though he was, he could not help noticing her beauty. She was the loveliest lady under the moon. When he saw the terror in her eyes, he was filled with compassion.

Goldborough would not even look at him. The thought of marrying a kitchen boy sickened her, yet she was too terrified to refuse. It must, she thought, be the will of God her creator, who sent the rain and the sunlight and made the corn grow.

Next morning they were married by the Archbishop of York.

NINE

Sheep and pigs we have and stores—
Oh stay with us, and all is yours!

As soon as they were married, Havelok and Goldborough fled from Godric, whose hatred was like a scorching fire. They went to Grimsby, for Havelok was longing to see Grim again.

But Grim had died in the famine. Nevertheless his family welcomed Havelok and Goldborough joyfully and were able for a while to forget their grief.

Havelok, however, was quite overcome with sorrow. He had been devoted to Grim.

'We are all of us well and prosperous again,' said Red Robert, the eldest son. 'Grim left us sheep and pigs, horses and cattle, a fishing boat——'

'Gold and silver too,' said William Wendut, the second son.

'He told us to share everything with you,' said Hugh Raven, the youngest son, whose eyes were as dark as a raven's wings. 'Stay with us and it will all be yours.'

'We will serve you and your lady faithfully,' said Dame Leve, their mother.

'Yes,' said Gunnild, the elder daughter. 'We will wash her clothes and wring them out, bring water for her hands, and prepare the bridal bed.'

'There is nothing we would like more than to have her for our lady,' said Levive, the younger daughter.

The three sons threw logs on to the fire, till it crackled and blazed and filled the room with good cheer. Then everyone sat down to a feast of chicken, goose, and duckling, which the women had prepared. They drank ale and sparkling wine and passed the wassail cup from lip to lip.

But in spite of all their efforts to please her, Goldborough remained unhappy. That night, as she lay in her bridal bed, she could not sleep. She could not forget that she was a princess and her husband only a kitchen boy. How cruelly Godric had disgraced her!

Suddenly she saw a light in the room, as bright as a hundred glittering candles. A shaft of brightness was streaming from Havelok's mouth, as he lay peacefully asleep at her side, and on his shoulder was a cross of gold. In the silence she heard an angel's voice speak to her to soothe her fears:

'Do not be sad, Goldborough. This golden cross proves that Havelok is no lowborn kitchen boy, but a King's son and heir. He will be King of Denmark and of England too, and you will be his Queen.'

At once her sadness melted away, and her face was as radiant as a sunlit peak. She kissed Havelok, and he awoke.

'Dearest Goldborough,' he said, brushing the sleep from his eyes, 'I have had the strangest dream. I dreamed I was in Denmark sitting on a hill, with the world stretched out at my feet. I leaned down to clutch hold of my country. My arms grew and grew, and soon I held all the towns and castles in my grasp. But when I tried to let go, everything clung to me. The castles bowed their heads, and their keys fell jingling at my feet.... Then I had another dream. I was flying over the sea to England, my people with me. I picked up England in my hand and gave it, dearest, to you. What can this dream mean?'

'It means that you will be crowned King of England as well as King of Denmark. Within a year every inch of Denmark will be yours. Every earl and baron, every knight, every townsman and peasant will hail you as King.'

'Then we must return to Denmark,' said Havelok.

'At once.' said Goldborough. 'And Grim's sons must go with us.'

'They may not agree to leave home.'

'They love you too well to stay behind.'

Next morning at dawn Havelok went straight to the chapel that Grim had built and knelt before the altar.

'Lord God,' he prayed, 'Almighty Ruler of the winds and waves, the woods and green fields, have mercy on me. Give me victory over my enemy Godard, who stabbed my sisters to death before my eyes, and who ordered Grim to drown me, though I never did him any harm. Calm my anxious mind. Keep me from storms and shipwreck, and bring me safely over to the sea to my country, to meet Godard face to face.'

He left an offering on the altar and went off to look for Grim's sons. They had planned to go fishing and were sorting their nets. He called them over to him and reminded them of how

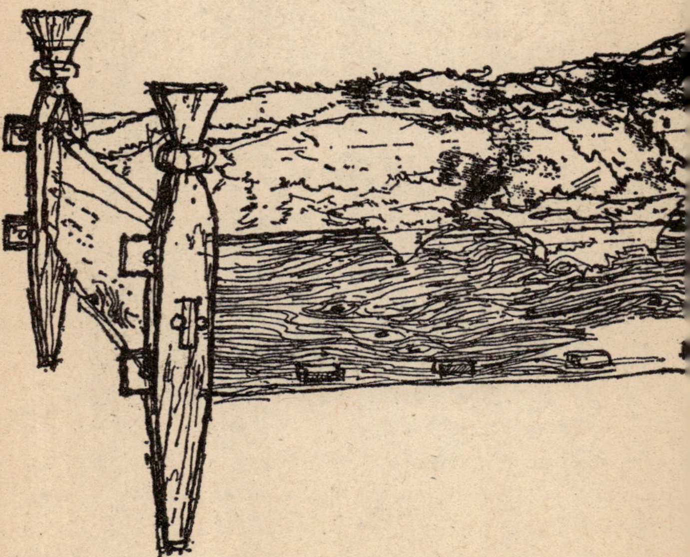

their father had years ago left Denmark and risked his life for Havelok's sake.

'The time has come now for me to return there,' said Havelok. 'If you will come with me, I will make you rich men. I will give each of you ten castles and all the lands, towns, woods, and fields that go with them. Dear brothers, I beg you to come.'

'I will go with you to the ends of the earth,' said Red Robert, on his knees.

'And I,' said William Wendut.

'And I,' said Hugh Raven.

TEN

Havelok's heart was full of dread
Lest she be hurt or blood be shed.

So Havelok, his wife Goldborough, and Grim's three sons set off for Denmark. They were already in sight of land when suddenly a pirate ship appeared. With flags flying and pipes blowing and bowmen by the mast, it closed in upon them—then suddenly turned aside and raced away. The pirates dared not grapple with Havelok, for they had seen a shaft of dazzling light above the mast, reaching up into the sky. The hand of God was over him, protecting him.

Havelok landed on a cliffless coast and asked for the castle of Duke Ubbe, the loyal friend of his father King Birkabeyn.

'Thirty miles to the south, in the Bay of Seals,' he was told.

As it was too late to go on, they spent the night ashore, then embarked again at dawn. With the wind behind them, they came quickly in sight of the thick walls of Duke Ubbe's stronghold. They found a landing place and went ashore.

A messenger had already warned the Duke that they were coming. At the head of a great company of knights and soldiers with threatening spears he rode out to meet them. But when he saw that the newcomers were unarmed and their ship was only a fishing smack, he ordered the spears to be lowered.

'Who are you, strangers?' he roared, and the sea wind sent his great beard streaming over his shoulders.

Havelok looked up at him and smiled. He knew that this was the man he was looking for.

'What do you want from me?' said the Duke.

'Permission to go from town to town selling my wares,' said Havelok. 'I am a merchant.'

He took a gold ring from his pocket and gave it to the Duke. It was worth every penny of a hundred pounds.

Once Duke Ubbe had slipped it on his finger, he would not have parted with it for the world. He beamed at Havelok and marvelled at his broad shoulders, his powerful chest, and tremendous height. Such a fellow ought not to be wasting his life peddling wares in the market place. He should be a knight, with shield and spear and shining armour. But he kept these thoughts to himself and said to Havelok, 'Your wishes, sir, are granted. Now you and your beautiful wife must come and dine with me in the castle.'

'I fear for my wife's safety, sir,' said Havelok. 'Your soldiers will not take their eyes off her.'

'I will see that she comes to no harm,' said the Duke.

He wheeled his horse and rode back to the castle. But before he had gone more than a few paces, he called out, loud enough for everyone to hear, 'You are both of you to come. Those are my wishes, and my orders.'

Havelok still felt uneasy, but he dared not

disobey. At least Robert the Red, William Wendut, and Hugh Raven were with him, and their presence comforted him. They would have given their lives for Goldborough.

ELEVEN

They spring, like hounds at a baited bear
With snarling fangs and teeth that tear.

As the guests entered the great hall of the castle, all eyes were on Havelok and Goldborough. Courteous and handsome, Havelok was a head taller than anyone else there. As for Goldborough, her beauty seemed to cast a spell on all who looked at her.

Duke Ubbe greeted them both with unaffected delight. Then he turned to his wife and said jokingly, 'You and Havelok can sit together. Goldborough can sit next to me. She is like a tulip tree in bloom—I swear there is no lovelier woman in all Denmark.'

His wife submitted gracefully. With Havelok beside her, she had to admit that her share of the bargain was quite as good.

After the chaplain had blessed the food, they all sat down to enjoy it. Swan, crane, venison, lamprey, sturgeon—no Emperor or King ever saw a more splendid feast. There was plenty of wine too. In that company even the smallest page would turn up his nose at mere ale.

When at last they had all finished and the wassail cup had been passed around many times, the Duke began to think about what he was going to do with his guests for the night. 'If they

leave without a guard, they are sure to be attacked,' he reflected. 'Someone will kill Havelok to get his wife.' He decided to send them to the house of his overseer, Bernard Brun, who was a brave and trustworthy knight.

So there they went, accompanied by a guard of ten knights and sixty swordsmen and bowmen to see that they came to no harm on the way.

Bernard Brun gave them a great welcome. Although they had hardly finished their dinner, he had prepared a handsome supper for them and he insisted on their doing justice to it. There was nothing mean or niggardly about Bernard Brun.

They had hardly sat down when there was a mighty battering on the hall door, and shouts of 'Unbar the door, Sir Bernard! Unbar the door! Or, by St. Augustine, we shall split you from chin to toe!'

Bernard Brun sprang to his feet and fastened on his coat of mail. Seizing a battle-axe, he rushed to the door, shouting above the din, 'Get out of my courtyard, you dirty thieves! if anyone comes near me, I'll knock his skull in, and I'll throw the rest of you into the dungeon.'

'Empty braggart!' cried a voice from the other side—the voice of a murderous ruffian, Griffin Galle. 'If you won't unbar the door, we'll break it down!'

He had hardly spoken when a great rock came crashing through the door, shattering the panels. Splinters went flying everywhere.

Havelok grabbed the door bar and wrenched it out of its brackets. What was left of the door once collapsed. But Havelok was standing there now, and he meant to put the door bar to good use.

The courtyard and street were full of ruffians, all of them yelling and waving swords or knives. Three of them sprang at Havelok. With a sideways swipe of the bar, he killed all three. The next man received the butt end in his right eye. Two stocky fellows behind him turned and ran, but they were not quick enough. He rammed one of them between the shoulder blades and broke the other's neck. A seventh man pointed his sword at Havelok's eye, but the bar caught him in the chest. In less time than it takes to run a mile, all seven were dead.

For a few moments the rest hung back. But when they saw that Havelok was now in the middle of the courtyard, alone and quite cut off from the hall, they drew their swords and rushed at him.

He was like a bear at the stake, surrounded by hounds trying to tear him to pieces. They threw stones at him, they clubbed him with great poles, they jabbed their swords into his back and sides. Soon he had more than twenty wounds. It was a miracle that he kept his feet. But he lopped them down with his bar, cracking every skull within reach, till twenty more had fallen. The remainder dropped back. Too scared to go near him, they took cover behind walls and gateposts, and pelted him with flints and spears.

Meanwhile Grim's three sons had been trying to break through the scrimmage at the door. But they could not get through. Then Hugh Raven,

grabbing an oar and a long knife, climbed the window sill, broke the glass, and jumped down into the courtyard.

'Robert! William! Where are you?' he shouted. 'Our master is in mortal danger!' He began to lay about him right and left with the oar.

His brothers heard his cry. In the moonlight they could see how hard pressed he was. Each grabbed a stake as thick as a man's thigh and ran out to help him, followed by Bernard Brun with his battle-axe. Three of them rushed at Havelok's attackers. They broke their ribs, they broke their arms, they broke their knees and legs and thighs till they were howling like babies in their cradles.

Soon the howling ended, for they were all dead.

TWELVE

... till you can walk again and ride
Your saddled palfrey, legs astride.

Next morning, as soon as Duke Ubbe heard of the attack on Havelok, he leaped on to his horse and galloped away with his knights to Bernard Brun's house. The street outside was full of dead bodies. Some were lying on the cobbles, others had been thrown into the ditch.

'Bernard, are you all right?' cried Duke Ubbe from the street.

There was a noise of banging and scraping as the barricade was removed from the shattered door. A man, nearly naked, came limping out. It was Bernard Brun.

'Sir, they hacked my armour and my clothes to pieces and left me nothing but these bruises,' said Bernard Brun.

Concerned for his friend, Duke Ubbe jumped down from his horse and grasped him by the shoulders.

'My lord, I am not badly hurt,' said Bernard. 'Havelok is much worse. He has a sword wound in his side and another in his arm. The gash in his thigh is the biggest I have ever seen. I'm afraid he may not live.'

The Duke's face was stricken with anxiety. 'Bring him to me at once, and send for a doctor,' he said.

'I have never seen a man fight as Havelok did,' said Bernard. 'I shall never forget it. In the middle of the night, just after moonrise, many ruffians sprang upon him. The murderer Griffin Galle was at their head. The only weapon Havelok had was a wooden bar. Without God's blessing, too, it never could have saved him. . . . Look, here he comes.'

The knights moved aside as Grim's three sons carried out a litter and laid it at the Duke's feet. Havelok was lying full length on it, his eyes closed, his cheeks as pale as parchment. Goldborough was kneeling in tears at his side.

'The doctor has arrived, my lord,' said Bernard.

A little man with a forked beard stepped forward. He lifted the cloak that covered Havelok and examined his wounds. He sponged away the blood and gently felt his bones. The Duke was so anxious for Havelok that he did not dare to look.

'He is badly hurt,' said the doctor. 'But no bones are broken and the wounds will heal in time. Yes, he will speak and walk and ride again as well as ever.'

'God be praised!' exclaimed the Duke. Over-

joyed, he comforted Goldborough and told her to dry her tears.

Havelok opened his eyes. When he saw Goldborough and the Duke, he smiled.

'I have heard what happened, Havelok, and shall knight you for your courage,' said the Duke. 'You and Goldborough must come at once to my castle, and your three servants too. You will be safe, for I shall give you a room next to my own.

There is only a wall of pinewood between them. I shall be able to hear every footstep, every whisper. You can come and see me whenever you like. You can stay in the castle till your wounds are healed and you are able to walk and ride again.'

So Havelok and Goldborough returned with the Duke to his castle. And with them went Red Robert, William Wendut, and Hugh Raven—three of the truest friends that a man could wish for.

THIRTEEN

Because you fought so brave a fight,
I honour you, and will dub you knight.

One night, some weeks later, Duke Ubbe woke suddenly and sat up in bed. Through the chinks in the pinewood wall that separated his room from Havelok's a bright light was shining. What was going on? Nobody except thieves and drunkards could be up at such an hour.

He got up and peered through a crack into the room. He could see Grim's three sons lying on the floor in sheepskin rugs, snoring. In the bed Havelok and Goldborough were fast asleep. A light as bright as a hundred glittering candles came from Havelok's mouth. What could it mean?

Duke Ubbe hurried downstairs to wake his knights and servants. He brought back more than a hundred of them to Havelok's room. The five sleepers had not woken. They were as motionless as carvings on a tomb. Havelok was lying on his left side, his lovely bride in his arms.

Then one of the knights noticed the mark on

Havelok's shoulder and asked what it was. They crowded round the bed.

'It's a kind of cross,' someone said.

'It sparkles like one of those jewelled crosses the Vikings brought from the Golden Horn,' said another.

'It is the birthmark of a King,' said Duke Ubbe. 'I had already noticed Havelok's resemblance to King Birkabeyn. This birthmark shows that he must be his son and heir.'

With tears of joy they all fell at Havelok's feet. They kissed the tips of his toes a hundred times. They were as overjoyed as if he had come back from the grave.

Havelok woke, like a tiger suddenly roused from sleep. He glowered angrily at them.

'We intend no harm, my lord,' said Duke Ubbe reassuringly. 'We have not come to attack you, but to kneel at your feet and pay homage to you. Tomorrow every man in this town shall follow our example. We have seen the proof that you are Birkabeyn's son and heir, the rightful King of Denmark.'

At once the frowning changed to smiles, and Havelok gave thanks to God.

Next morning Duke Ubbe sent a herald to summon his people—every earl and baron, every priest in Holy Orders, every thane and knight and peasant in the town. They gathered in the market place, where he addressed them from a balcony. He told them of the promise that

Godard had made when King Birkabeyn lay dying. He told them how it had been broken, and the King's daughters had both been killed. Thanks to God's mercy Havelok was still alive. He told them how Grim had taken him to England and looked after him till he grew to manhood.

'Now Havelok has returned to Denmark,' he ended. 'You will find him tall and brave and handsome—there is no one in all the world to match him. Here he is!'

The door behind him opened and Havelok stepped out on to the balcony. Duke Ubbe knelt, the first to do him homage. In words that everyone could hear, he swore to be his man.

There was a moment of stunned silence. Then a serving man in the crowd began to cheer. Another waved and shouted that he was Havelok's man. Soon everyone was cheering and shouting for Havelok. By sunset there was not a man in the town, rich or poor, bondman or free, who had not sworn allegiance to him.

That same day Duke Ubbe sent messengers to summon to the castle every governor, constable, and sheriff in the land. No one failed to come, for they were afraid of Duke Ubbe. On the appointed day they all took the oath of allegiance. After the ceremony the Duke presented Havelok to them. He drew his sword and knighted him. Then he named him King of Denmark and gave all the people into his care.

Havelok's first action as King was to reward Grim's sons. He gave them each a knightood, together with lands and possessions and a retinue of twenty knights. Then he ordered forty days of

feasting and celebration. There were gay tournaments, with charging horses, much splintering of lances, and clashing of swords. There was wrestling and putting the stone, bullfights and

bear-baiting. At night every hall in the land rang to the music of minstrels, with drum and tabor, harp and tambourine. There were jesters and jugglers, ballad-singers and tellers of tales. In all the world there was no happier kingdom than Havelok's.

FOURTEEN

Tight they bound him, nose to tail,
With rope from an ancient fishing sail.

When the celebrations were over and Havelok had taken possession of all the castles in the land, he sent fifty specially picked fighting men, with Red Robert in command, to search for Godard.

They found him in the forest, hunting the wild boar. Power had made him so sure of himself, so stiff-necked and arrogant, that he seemed quite blind to all that had been happening.

Red Robert galloped up to him and shouted fearlessly, 'Traitor, I arrest you in the King's name.'

'The King?' said Godard, pretending not to understand. 'In Denmark it is I who give the orders.'

'You know very well who I mean,' said Red Robert. 'Everybody knows how you treated Havelok and killed his sisters. The King would like to give you your reward.'

'First let me give you *your* reward,' said

Godard. And he smashed his fist into Red Robert's face.

Robert whipped out his knife and stabbed him in the arm. It fell limply at his side so that Godard could not strike again.

Godard's horse reared and wildly pawed the air.

'Kill these traitors!' he shouted to his men.

But they flinched when they saw the look on Red Robert's face. And when William Wendut, Hugh Raven, and five others came galloping up, they turned and fled.

'Miserable cowards!' cried Godard. 'Why do you desert me in my hour of need? Have you forgotten that you swore allegiance to me, that I have fed you and looked after you all your lives? It is your sacred duty to help me now.'

His words shamed them into returning. But they dared not go near Red Robert. Sheltering behind the trees, they shot their arrows, killing a knight and a peasant and wounding ten others. But the rest of Red Robert's party swooped down on them and slew them to a man. Godard alone was left alive.

They bound him hand and foot, pulling the cords so tightly that they cut into his flesh. And how he roared! He sounded like a bull trapped in the corner of a field, with hounds baiting him on every side. They bundled him on to a scabby rawboned mare, nose to tail, and drove him away to Havelok.

In spite of all the misery and suffering Godard had heaped on him, Havelok insisted on giving his prisoner a fair trial. In Duke Ubbe's hall, before a huge gathering, the judges gave their verdict: 'We pronounce Godard guilty. He shall be beaten with rods, then tied to a mare's tail and dragged across the fields to the gallows, to be hanged in chains. In the gallows-beam above his head these words shall be carved: THE MURDERER OF INNOCENT CHILDREN, THE TRAITOR WHO STOLE A KINGDOM. That is our sentence. We have no more to say.'

FIFTEEN

Shall we let them rob us of our lives,
Enslave our children, kill our wives?

After Havelok had been reigning in Denmark for four years, Goldborough asked him to take her back to England to claim her kingdom. Havelock agreed and, as soon as the wind was fair, he set sail with a fleet of four hundred and eighty ships. They landed at Grimsby and pitched their tents near the harbour.

After the cramped and cheerless voyage over the North Sea the soldiers were cold and hungry. Havelok's first concern was to feed them and see to their welfare. Next he started to build an abbey. It was to be called Grimsby Abbey, in memory of the man who had been friend and father to him when he was young and helpless.

Godric was in Lincoln when he heard of Goldborough's return to England. In great agitation he paced up and down the stone floors of the castle, shouting, 'Does she think she can rob me of my throne? I'll see her hanged first!'

At once he set about gathering an army. Every

man who could ride a horse and carry a shield and spear—even an axe or a scythe—was ordered to assemble in Lincoln square on March 17th. The punishment for disobedience was slavery. But no one disobeyed. They were terrified of Godric.

'I have not brought you here for sport,' he told them. 'Danish invaders have landed at Grismby and seized the priory. They are plundering the villages, setting fire to churches, strangling monks and nuns. Soon they will be killing us, our wives and children too, unless we stop them. Will you help me to drive them away?' He drew his sword and waved it in the air. 'My sword will be the first to taste Danish blood. You must follow wherever it leads. Then we shall sweep these dogs from the land.'

'We'll follow you!' cried Earl Gunter.

'We will! We will!' cried Reyner, Earl of Chester.

The whole army burst into cheering. They put on their armour, sprang into the saddle, and rode off for Grimsby, mad for battle.

But Havelok's scouts were quick to report their movements. By the time the advance party reached Grimsby, he was ready. He it was that struck the first blow, beheading a knight who tried to knock him from the saddle. Red Robert struck the next; he killed a baron who had an orange banner streaming from his spear. The third victim fell to William Wendut. He struck

the fellow below the left shoulder, and arm and shield went flying off together. An earl fighting beside him tried to gallop from the field, but Hugh Raven caught him and cleft his head in two.

Levelling his spear, Duke Ubbe charged at Godric. They collided so violently that both were hurled headlong from the saddle. They leaped up from the ground, drew their swords, and began to hack madly at each other. All day long they fought, while the sweat streamed down their armour. At sunset Godric at last succeeded in wounding the Duke in the side. He would have beheaded him had not Hugh Raven dragged him to safety. Already more than a thousand knights on both sides had fallen. The battle raged all over the field.

Little by little Godric drove the Danes back, killing every man within reach. They went down like grass before a scythe.

When Havelok saw that none of his men could stand up to Godric, he galloped up to him and shouted, 'Traitor and murderer! You have slaughtered my bravest knights! You have broken your oath to King Athelwold! Give Goldborough the land which is hers by right, then I will forgive you.'

'Never!' cried Godric. 'She shall be hanged. As for you, Havelok, here is my answer——'

He raised his sword and brought it crashing down onto Havelok's shield, cleaving it in two.

Then Havelok struck a mighty blow at Godric's helmet, so that the earl lost his balance and fell to the ground. But he sprang up at once and, as Havelok dismounted, slashed at his shoulder, stripping the rings from his coat of mail and cutting deep into the flesh.

Havelok gasped. His cheeks were red with shame and anger, red as the blood pouring from his wound. With a huge effort he heaved up his sword, then cut off Godric's right hand. He seized him by the throat, and had him bound in chains and sent to the Queen.

'Guard him carefully,' he told her. 'But let no one lift a finger against him. I have already disgraced him in front of his army. Now we must leave him to the judges.'

SIXTEEN

For she is fair and she is free
And rich in grace and courtesy.

After the capture of Godric, the English army at once surrendered. Then Havelok introduced Goldborough to her countrymen. He wanted them to be sure they recognized her before accepting her as Queen. Six earls stepped forward to greet her. They knew her at once, for she was the loveliest and gentlest lady under the sun. Weeping bitterly, they knelt and kissed her hand. Then the whole army knelt.

'Lady, we have treated you shamefully and beg you to forgive us,' said Earl Gunter. 'All England is now yours and we are your men.'

'The traitor Godric had no right to the kingdom,' said the Earl of Chester. 'He must be hanged.'

'That is for the judges to decide,' said Havelok. 'When they have given their verdict, I will accept your homage and take your oaths of allegiance.'

The trial began at once. The judges' verdict

was that Godric should be lashed to a donkey's back, with his nose to its tail, dragged off to Lincoln, and burned at the stake.

So a great wrong was avenged. Goldborough was crowned Queen of England and Havelok became King.

As soon as he had taken the oaths of allegiance, he rewarded all those who had helped him. Grim's daughters were still unmarried, and he wanted to see them happily and prosperously settled. At his suggestion the Earl of Chester, a handsome young bachelor, married the elder daughter, the courteous and gracious Gunnild. Levive, the younger, married Bertram, the Earl of Lincoln's cook, who now became Duke of Cornwall.

'I have never forgotten your kindness, Bertram,' said Havelok. 'When I was starving you took me in and saved my life. You could not wish for a better or more beautiful wife than Levive. Her cheeks are like roses when the sun first opens them. Treat her as kindly as you treated me.'

After the Danes had received their share of rewards, Havelok marched his army south to London. A coronation feast was held, and the celebrations lasted more than forty days. Afterward the Danes asked for leave to return to Denmark, and he allowed them to go. Duke Ubbe went with them, to rule the country in Havelok's place.

Havelok never returned to Denmark, for he

could not bear to be parted from his wife. For sixty winters they ruled England together. They loved each other so tenderly that no angry word ever passed between them. They had fifteen children, and all their sons became Kings and all their daughters Queens.

THE BLACK PEARL *by Scott O'Dell* 20p
552 52008 X Carousel Fiction

The Black Pearl belonged to the old men, with legends and stories to tell to pass the time—or so Ramon Salazar had thought, until he came face to face with the devilfish and the struggle for the pearl began. But Ramon had more than the dangers of the sea to conquer. Others wanted the Great Pearl of Heaven, including the evil Pearler from Seville.

THE STORY OF MAUDE REED *by Norah Lofts* 25p
552 52010 1 Carousel Fiction

Her grandfather was only a wool merchant and his house was not considered suitable for a young girl of noble blood. Maude was now old enough to be taught the accomplishments of a lady; sewing, music and the art of graceful behaviour. But this was the fifteenth century, and her school was to be an old, dark castle.

THE STORY OF BRITAIN (4 vols) each 30p
by R. J. Unstead
552 54001 3 552 54003 X Carousel Non-Fiction
552 54002 1 552 54004 8

A country is forged by its history, the battles and intrigues of bygone ages laying the foundations of today. From its beginnings as an island to the end of the Second World War, this series is the record of the men and women who played a role in shaping the character of England now. It traces the emergence of England as a nation.